50 Premium Cereal Recipes

By: Kelly Johnson

Table of Contents

- Honey Almond Crunch Granola
- Dark Chocolate & Sea Salt Oat Clusters
- Maple Pecan Protein Cereal
- Coconut Chia Crunch Cereal
- Vanilla Bean & Blueberry Muesli
- Cinnamon Apple Pie Granola
- Pistachio & Rosewater Honey Puffs
- Golden Turmeric Superfood Cereal
- Pumpkin Spice & Walnut Oat Clusters
- Matcha Green Tea & Almond Flakes
- Caramelized Banana Nut Cereal
- Hazelnut Mocha Crunch Granola
- Toasted Coconut & Mango Oat Cereal
- Lavender Honey & Almond Muesli
- Spiced Pear & Pecan Crunch Cereal
- Chocolate Hazelnut & Espresso Granola
- Lemon Poppy Seed Oat Clusters
- Salted Caramel & Cashew Cereal
- Berry Bliss Chia & Flax Granola
- Maple Bacon & Walnut Cereal
- Cherry Almond & Dark Chocolate Muesli
- Gingerbread Spice & Molasses Granola
- Tropical Coconut & Pineapple Crunch
- Vanilla Bourbon & Macadamia Nut Cereal
- Roasted Fig & Cinnamon Oat Cereal
- Peanut Butter & Jelly Crunch Clusters
- Cranberry Orange & Pecan Muesli
- Honey Lavender & Pistachio Cereal
- Chai Spiced Almond & Coconut Flakes
- Espresso Bean & Hazelnut Crunch Cereal
- Almond Butter & Dark Chocolate Granola
- Strawberry Shortcake Oat Cereal
- Coconut Carrot Cake Crunch Cereal
- Chocolate Peanut Butter Banana Clusters
- Salted Maple & Walnut Oat Cereal

- Mango Lassi Yogurt Cereal Clusters
- Cinnamon Raisin Swirl Granola
- Tahini Date & Sesame Crunch Cereal
- Raspberry White Chocolate Granola
- Chili Chocolate & Almond Crunch Cereal
- Toasted Pecan & Brown Butter Granola
- Tropical Passionfruit & Macadamia Cereal
- Espresso & Dark Chocolate Almond Muesli
- Pumpkin Seed & Spiced Honey Crunch
- Blackberry & Lavender Oat Cereal
- Ginger Almond & Cranberry Clusters
- Hazelnut Praline & Caramelized Oat Cereal
- Pineapple Coconut & Cashew Crunch
- Chili Lime & Coconut Flake Cereal
- Pistachio & Cardamom Spiced Granola

Honey Almond Crunch Granola

Ingredients:

- 2 cups rolled oats
- 1/2 cup sliced almonds
- 1/4 cup honey
- 2 tbsp coconut oil, melted
- 1/2 tsp vanilla extract
- 1/2 tsp cinnamon

Instructions:

1. Preheat oven to 325°F (165°C).
2. Mix oats, almonds, cinnamon, honey, coconut oil, and vanilla.
3. Spread on a baking sheet and bake for 20 minutes, stirring halfway.
4. Let cool before serving.

Dark Chocolate & Sea Salt Oat Clusters

Ingredients:

- 2 cups rolled oats
- 1/2 cup dark chocolate chunks
- 1/4 cup maple syrup
- 2 tbsp coconut oil, melted
- 1/2 tsp sea salt

Instructions:

1. Mix oats, maple syrup, coconut oil, and salt.
2. Spread on a baking sheet and bake at 325°F (165°C) for 15 minutes.
3. Let cool and stir in dark chocolate chunks.

Maple Pecan Protein Cereal

Ingredients:

- 2 cups rolled oats
- 1/2 cup chopped pecans
- 1/4 cup maple syrup
- 2 tbsp protein powder (vanilla or unflavored)
- 1 tbsp coconut oil

Instructions:

1. Mix oats, pecans, maple syrup, protein powder, and coconut oil.
2. Bake at 325°F (165°C) for 15 minutes, stirring halfway.

Coconut Chia Crunch Cereal

Ingredients:

- 2 cups shredded coconut
- 1/4 cup chia seeds
- 1/4 cup honey
- 2 tbsp coconut oil
- 1/2 tsp cinnamon

Instructions:

1. Mix coconut, chia seeds, honey, coconut oil, and cinnamon.
2. Spread on a baking sheet and bake at 300°F (150°C) for 12 minutes.

Vanilla Bean & Blueberry Muesli

Ingredients:

- 2 cups rolled oats
- 1/2 cup dried blueberries
- 1/4 cup sliced almonds
- 1 tsp vanilla bean powder
- 1 tbsp honey

Instructions:

1. Mix oats, blueberries, almonds, and vanilla bean powder.
2. Drizzle honey over and mix well before serving.

Cinnamon Apple Pie Granola

Ingredients:

- 2 cups rolled oats
- 1/2 cup dried apple slices, chopped
- 1/4 cup chopped walnuts
- 1/4 cup honey
- 1 tsp cinnamon

Instructions:

1. Mix oats, apples, walnuts, honey, and cinnamon.
2. Bake at 325°F (165°C) for 20 minutes.

Pistachio & Rosewater Honey Puffs

Ingredients:

- 2 cups puffed rice or quinoa
- 1/4 cup chopped pistachios
- 2 tbsp honey
- 1/2 tsp rosewater

Instructions:

1. Mix puffed rice, pistachios, honey, and rosewater.
2. Bake at 300°F (150°C) for 10 minutes.

Golden Turmeric Superfood Cereal

Ingredients:

- 2 cups rolled oats
- 1/4 cup shredded coconut
- 1/2 tsp turmeric
- 1/2 tsp cinnamon
- 1 tbsp honey

Instructions:

1. Mix oats, coconut, turmeric, cinnamon, and honey.
2. Bake at 325°F (165°C) for 15 minutes.

Pumpkin Spice & Walnut Oat Clusters

Ingredients:

- 2 cups rolled oats
- 1/2 cup chopped walnuts
- 1/4 cup pumpkin puree
- 1 tbsp maple syrup
- 1 tsp pumpkin spice

Instructions:

1. Mix oats, walnuts, pumpkin, maple syrup, and pumpkin spice.
2. Bake at 325°F (165°C) for 15 minutes.

Matcha Green Tea & Almond Flakes

Ingredients:

- 2 cups rolled oats
- 1/2 cup sliced almonds
- 1 tbsp matcha powder
- 1 tbsp honey

Instructions:

1. Mix oats, almonds, matcha, and honey.
2. Bake at 300°F (150°C) for 12 minutes.

Caramelized Banana Nut Cereal

Ingredients:

- 2 cups rolled oats
- 1/2 cup chopped walnuts
- 1 ripe banana, mashed
- 2 tbsp honey
- 1 tbsp coconut oil
- 1/2 tsp cinnamon

Instructions:

1. Preheat oven to 325°F (165°C).
2. Mix oats, walnuts, banana, honey, coconut oil, and cinnamon.
3. Spread on a baking sheet and bake for 20 minutes, stirring halfway.

Hazelnut Mocha Crunch Granola

Ingredients:

- 2 cups rolled oats
- 1/2 cup chopped hazelnuts
- 1 tbsp cocoa powder
- 1 tbsp instant espresso powder
- 1/4 cup maple syrup
- 2 tbsp coconut oil

Instructions:

1. Mix oats, hazelnuts, cocoa powder, and espresso powder.
2. Stir in maple syrup and coconut oil.
3. Bake at 325°F (165°C) for 15–20 minutes.

Toasted Coconut & Mango Oat Cereal

Ingredients:

- 2 cups rolled oats
- 1/2 cup shredded coconut
- 1/2 cup dried mango, chopped
- 2 tbsp honey
- 1 tbsp coconut oil

Instructions:

1. Mix oats, coconut, honey, and coconut oil.
2. Bake at 300°F (150°C) for 12 minutes.
3. Stir in dried mango after baking.

Lavender Honey & Almond Muesli

Ingredients:

- 2 cups rolled oats
- 1/2 cup sliced almonds
- 1/2 tsp dried lavender
- 2 tbsp honey

Instructions:

1. Mix oats, almonds, and lavender.
2. Drizzle with honey before serving.

Spiced Pear & Pecan Crunch Cereal

Ingredients:

- 2 cups rolled oats
- 1/2 cup chopped pecans
- 1/2 cup dried pear, chopped
- 1/2 tsp cinnamon
- 1/4 tsp nutmeg
- 2 tbsp maple syrup

Instructions:

1. Mix oats, pecans, cinnamon, nutmeg, and maple syrup.
2. Bake at 325°F (165°C) for 15 minutes.
3. Stir in dried pear after baking.

Chocolate Hazelnut & Espresso Granola

Ingredients:

- 2 cups rolled oats
- 1/2 cup chopped hazelnuts
- 1 tbsp cocoa powder
- 1 tbsp espresso powder
- 2 tbsp honey
- 1 tbsp coconut oil

Instructions:

1. Mix oats, hazelnuts, cocoa powder, and espresso powder.
2. Stir in honey and coconut oil.
3. Bake at 325°F (165°C) for 15–20 minutes.

Lemon Poppy Seed Oat Clusters

Ingredients:

- 2 cups rolled oats
- 1 tbsp poppy seeds
- Zest of 1 lemon
- 2 tbsp honey
- 1 tbsp coconut oil

Instructions:

1. Mix oats, poppy seeds, lemon zest, honey, and coconut oil.
2. Bake at 300°F (150°C) for 12 minutes.

Salted Caramel & Cashew Cereal

Ingredients:

- 2 cups rolled oats
- 1/2 cup chopped cashews
- 2 tbsp caramel sauce
- 1/2 tsp sea salt

Instructions:

1. Mix oats, cashews, caramel sauce, and sea salt.
2. Bake at 325°F (165°C) for 15 minutes.

Berry Bliss Chia & Flax Granola

Ingredients:

- 2 cups rolled oats
- 1/4 cup chia seeds
- 1/4 cup flaxseeds
- 1/2 cup dried mixed berries
- 2 tbsp honey
- 1 tbsp coconut oil

Instructions:

1. Mix oats, chia seeds, flaxseeds, honey, and coconut oil.
2. Bake at 300°F (150°C) for 12 minutes.
3. Stir in dried berries after baking.

Maple Bacon & Walnut Cereal

Ingredients:

- 2 cups rolled oats
- 1/2 cup chopped walnuts
- 4 strips crispy bacon, crumbled
- 2 tbsp maple syrup

Instructions:

1. Mix oats, walnuts, and maple syrup.
2. Bake at 325°F (165°C) for 15 minutes.
3. Stir in crumbled bacon after baking.

Cherry Almond & Dark Chocolate Muesli

Ingredients:

- 2 cups rolled oats
- 1/2 cup dried cherries
- 1/2 cup sliced almonds
- 1/4 cup dark chocolate chunks
- 1 tbsp honey

Instructions:

1. Mix oats, cherries, and almonds.
2. Stir in honey and mix well.
3. Add dark chocolate chunks before serving.

Gingerbread Spice & Molasses Granola

Ingredients:

- 2 cups rolled oats
- 1/2 cup chopped pecans
- 1/4 cup molasses
- 1 tsp ground ginger
- 1/2 tsp cinnamon
- 1/4 tsp nutmeg
- 2 tbsp coconut oil

Instructions:

1. Mix oats, pecans, ginger, cinnamon, and nutmeg.
2. Stir in molasses and coconut oil.
3. Bake at 325°F (165°C) for 15–20 minutes.

Tropical Coconut & Pineapple Crunch

Ingredients:

- 2 cups rolled oats
- 1/2 cup shredded coconut
- 1/2 cup dried pineapple, chopped
- 2 tbsp honey
- 1 tbsp coconut oil

Instructions:

1. Mix oats, coconut, honey, and coconut oil.
2. Bake at 300°F (150°C) for 12 minutes.
3. Stir in dried pineapple after baking.

Vanilla Bourbon & Macadamia Nut Cereal

Ingredients:

- 2 cups rolled oats
- 1/2 cup chopped macadamia nuts
- 1 tsp vanilla extract
- 1 tbsp bourbon
- 2 tbsp maple syrup

Instructions:

1. Mix oats, macadamia nuts, vanilla, bourbon, and maple syrup.
2. Bake at 325°F (165°C) for 15 minutes.

Roasted Fig & Cinnamon Oat Cereal

Ingredients:

- 2 cups rolled oats
- 1/2 cup chopped roasted figs
- 1/2 tsp cinnamon
- 2 tbsp honey

Instructions:

1. Mix oats, cinnamon, and honey.
2. Bake at 325°F (165°C) for 15 minutes.
3. Stir in roasted figs after baking.

Peanut Butter & Jelly Crunch Clusters

Ingredients:

- 2 cups rolled oats
- 1/4 cup peanut butter, melted
- 1/4 cup dried strawberries or raspberries
- 2 tbsp honey

Instructions:

1. Mix oats, peanut butter, and honey.
2. Bake at 300°F (150°C) for 12 minutes.
3. Stir in dried fruit after baking.

Cranberry Orange & Pecan Muesli

Ingredients:

- 2 cups rolled oats
- 1/2 cup dried cranberries
- 1/2 cup chopped pecans
- Zest of 1 orange
- 1 tbsp honey

Instructions:

1. Mix oats, cranberries, pecans, and orange zest.
2. Stir in honey before serving.

Honey Lavender & Pistachio Cereal

Ingredients:

- 2 cups rolled oats
- 1/2 cup chopped pistachios
- 1/2 tsp dried lavender
- 2 tbsp honey

Instructions:

1. Mix oats, pistachios, and lavender.
2. Stir in honey before serving.

Chai Spiced Almond & Coconut Flakes

Ingredients:

- 2 cups rolled oats
- 1/2 cup sliced almonds
- 1/2 cup coconut flakes
- 1 tsp chai spice mix
- 2 tbsp maple syrup

Instructions:

1. Mix oats, almonds, coconut, and chai spice.
2. Stir in maple syrup.
3. Bake at 325°F (165°C) for 15 minutes.

Espresso Bean & Hazelnut Crunch Cereal

Ingredients:

- 2 cups rolled oats
- 1/2 cup chopped hazelnuts
- 1 tbsp finely ground espresso beans
- 2 tbsp honey

Instructions:

1. Mix oats, hazelnuts, and ground espresso.
2. Stir in honey.
3. Bake at 325°F (165°C) for 15 minutes.

Almond Butter & Dark Chocolate Granola

Ingredients:

- 2 cups rolled oats
- 1/2 cup sliced almonds
- 1/4 cup almond butter
- 2 tbsp honey
- 1/2 tsp cinnamon
- 1/4 cup dark chocolate chunks

Instructions:

1. Preheat oven to 325°F (165°C).
2. Mix oats, almonds, almond butter, honey, and cinnamon.
3. Spread on a baking sheet and bake for 15–20 minutes.
4. Let cool and stir in dark chocolate chunks.

Strawberry Shortcake Oat Cereal

Ingredients:

- 2 cups rolled oats
- 1/2 cup freeze-dried strawberries
- 1/2 cup crushed vanilla wafers
- 2 tbsp honey
- 1 tsp vanilla extract

Instructions:

1. Mix oats, honey, and vanilla extract.
2. Bake at 300°F (150°C) for 12 minutes.
3. Stir in freeze-dried strawberries and vanilla wafers after baking.

Coconut Carrot Cake Crunch Cereal

Ingredients:

- 2 cups rolled oats
- 1/2 cup shredded coconut
- 1/2 cup grated carrot
- 1/4 cup chopped pecans
- 2 tbsp honey
- 1/2 tsp cinnamon

Instructions:

1. Mix oats, coconut, carrot, pecans, honey, and cinnamon.
2. Bake at 325°F (165°C) for 15 minutes.

Chocolate Peanut Butter Banana Clusters

Ingredients:

- 2 cups rolled oats
- 1/2 cup peanut butter
- 1 mashed banana
- 1/4 cup dark chocolate chips
- 1 tbsp honey

Instructions:

1. Mix oats, peanut butter, mashed banana, and honey.
2. Form small clusters and bake at 300°F (150°C) for 12 minutes.
3. Stir in chocolate chips after baking.

Salted Maple & Walnut Oat Cereal

Ingredients:

- 2 cups rolled oats
- 1/2 cup chopped walnuts
- 2 tbsp maple syrup
- 1/2 tsp sea salt

Instructions:

1. Mix oats, walnuts, maple syrup, and sea salt.
2. Bake at 325°F (165°C) for 15 minutes.

Mango Lassi Yogurt Cereal Clusters

Ingredients:

- 2 cups rolled oats
- 1/2 cup dried mango, chopped
- 1/2 cup Greek yogurt
- 1 tbsp honey
- 1/2 tsp ground cardamom

Instructions:

1. Mix oats, Greek yogurt, honey, and cardamom.
2. Form clusters and bake at 300°F (150°C) for 12 minutes.
3. Stir in dried mango after baking.

Cinnamon Raisin Swirl Granola

Ingredients:

- 2 cups rolled oats
- 1/2 cup raisins
- 1/4 cup chopped walnuts
- 2 tbsp honey
- 1 tsp cinnamon

Instructions:

1. Mix oats, walnuts, honey, and cinnamon.
2. Bake at 325°F (165°C) for 15 minutes.
3. Stir in raisins after baking.

Tahini Date & Sesame Crunch Cereal

Ingredients:

- 2 cups rolled oats
- 1/2 cup chopped dates
- 2 tbsp tahini
- 1 tbsp honey
- 2 tbsp sesame seeds

Instructions:

1. Mix oats, tahini, honey, and sesame seeds.
2. Bake at 300°F (150°C) for 12 minutes.
3. Stir in chopped dates after baking.

Raspberry White Chocolate Granola

Ingredients:

- 2 cups rolled oats
- 1/2 cup freeze-dried raspberries
- 1/4 cup white chocolate chunks
- 2 tbsp honey

Instructions:

1. Mix oats and honey.
2. Bake at 300°F (150°C) for 12 minutes.
3. Stir in raspberries and white chocolate after baking.

Chili Chocolate & Almond Crunch Cereal

Ingredients:

- 2 cups rolled oats
- 1/2 cup sliced almonds
- 1/4 cup dark chocolate chunks
- 1/2 tsp chili powder
- 2 tbsp honey
- 1 tbsp coconut oil

Instructions:

1. Mix oats, almonds, chili powder, honey, and coconut oil.
2. Bake at 325°F (165°C) for 15 minutes.
3. Stir in dark chocolate chunks after baking.

Toasted Pecan & Brown Butter Granola

Ingredients:

- 2 cups rolled oats
- 1/2 cup chopped pecans
- 2 tbsp brown butter
- 1/4 cup maple syrup
- 1/2 tsp cinnamon

Instructions:

1. Toast pecans in brown butter.
2. Mix oats, pecans, maple syrup, and cinnamon.
3. Bake at 325°F (165°C) for 15 minutes.

Tropical Passionfruit & Macadamia Cereal

Ingredients:

- 2 cups rolled oats
- 1/2 cup chopped macadamia nuts
- 1/4 cup dried passionfruit pieces
- 2 tbsp honey

Instructions:

1. Mix oats, macadamia nuts, and honey.
2. Bake at 300°F (150°C) for 12 minutes.
3. Stir in dried passionfruit after baking.

Espresso & Dark Chocolate Almond Muesli

Ingredients:

- 2 cups rolled oats
- 1/2 cup sliced almonds
- 1 tbsp finely ground espresso beans
- 1/4 cup dark chocolate chunks
- 1 tbsp honey

Instructions:

1. Mix oats, almonds, espresso, and honey.
2. Stir in dark chocolate chunks before serving.

Pumpkin Seed & Spiced Honey Crunch

Ingredients:

- 2 cups rolled oats
- 1/2 cup pumpkin seeds
- 1/4 cup honey
- 1/2 tsp cinnamon
- 1/4 tsp nutmeg

Instructions:

1. Mix oats, pumpkin seeds, honey, cinnamon, and nutmeg.
2. Bake at 325°F (165°C) for 15 minutes.

Blackberry & Lavender Oat Cereal

Ingredients:

- 2 cups rolled oats
- 1/2 cup freeze-dried blackberries
- 1/2 tsp dried lavender
- 2 tbsp honey

Instructions:

1. Mix oats, lavender, and honey.
2. Bake at 300°F (150°C) for 12 minutes.
3. Stir in blackberries after baking.

Ginger Almond & Cranberry Clusters

Ingredients:

- 2 cups rolled oats
- 1/2 cup sliced almonds
- 1/2 cup dried cranberries
- 1/2 tsp ground ginger
- 2 tbsp honey

Instructions:

1. Mix oats, almonds, ginger, and honey.
2. Bake at 300°F (150°C) for 12 minutes.
3. Stir in cranberries after baking.

Hazelnut Praline & Caramelized Oat Cereal

Ingredients:

- 2 cups rolled oats
- 1/2 cup chopped hazelnuts
- 1/4 cup caramel sauce
- 2 tbsp brown sugar

Instructions:

1. Mix oats, hazelnuts, caramel sauce, and brown sugar.
2. Bake at 325°F (165°C) for 15 minutes.

Pineapple Coconut & Cashew Crunch

Ingredients:

- 2 cups rolled oats
- 1/2 cup shredded coconut
- 1/2 cup dried pineapple, chopped
- 1/2 cup cashews
- 2 tbsp honey

Instructions:

1. Mix oats, coconut, cashews, and honey.
2. Bake at 300°F (150°C) for 12 minutes.
3. Stir in dried pineapple after baking.

Chili Lime & Coconut Flake Cereal

Ingredients:

- 2 cups rolled oats
- 1/2 cup coconut flakes
- Zest of 1 lime
- 1/2 tsp chili powder
- 2 tbsp honey

Instructions:

1. Mix oats, coconut, lime zest, chili powder, and honey.
2. Bake at 300°F (150°C) for 12 minutes.

Pistachio & Cardamom Spiced Granola

Ingredients:

- 2 cups rolled oats
- 1/2 cup chopped pistachios
- 1/2 tsp ground cardamom
- 2 tbsp honey

Instructions:

1. Mix oats, pistachios, cardamom, and honey.
2. Bake at 325°F (165°C) for 15 minutes.

www.ingramcontent.com/pod-product-compliance
Lightning Source LLC
LaVergne TN
LVHW061956070526
838199LV00060B/4145